Dracula

The Origins of the Myth and Legend

Conrad Bauer

Copyrights

All rights reserved © 2018 by Conrad Bauer and Maplewood Publishing. No part of this publication or the information in it may be quoted from or reproduced in any form by means such as printing, scanning, photocopying, or otherwise without prior written permission of the copyright holder.

Disclaimer and Terms of Use

Efforts has been made to ensure that the information in this book is accurate and complete. However, the author and the publisher do not warrant the accuracy of the information, text, and graphics contained within the book due to the rapidly changing nature of science, research, known and unknown facts, and internet. The author and the publisher do not hold any responsibility for errors, omissions, or contrary interpretation of the subject matter herein. This book is presented solely for motivational and informational purposes only

ISBN: 978-1987412673

Printed in the United States

www.maplewoodpublishing.com

Contents

Introduction _____ 1

Did Dracula Really Exist? _____ 3

The Precarious Childhood of Dracula _____ 5

Dracula and the Tightrope of Leadership _____ 13

Dracula Takes Back His Throne _____ 19

Beating the Drums of War _____ 25

The Dragon's Crusade _____ 35

Vlad Dracula's Escape _____ 41

The Return of the Dark Prince _____ 47

The Death of Dracula? _____ 51

Persisting Myths and Legends of Dracula _____ 57

The Compelling Haunting of Dracula _____ 65

Also by Conrad Bauer _____ 67

Further Readings _____ 71

Introduction

He has been called by many names. He was the Prince, Vlad III; he was the Dark Lord, Vlad Dracula, and the terrible scourge, Vlad the Impaler. He had some rather heady titles considering he was just a minor ruler of a small, remote territory in southeastern Europe called Wallachia. But Vlad Dracula's land and reign, although small, would prove to be pivotal since his territory had become the stepping stone and beachhead of invasion for the mightiest Islamic force the world has ever known; the Ottoman Empire.

Vlad's tiny kingdom was one of the last Balkan countries to be conquered by the Ottoman Turks. It had been reduced to a vassal status and forced to pay tribute to the sultan, but it still maintained its autonomy. Stuck between a rock and a hard place, Vlad was born into a world where double dealing and Machiavellian strategy were second nature. During his early reign he was fully capable of paying the Ottoman sultan tribute while simultaneously promising the Christian powers of Hungary and Austria that he would soon join them in a holy war against the Ottoman Empire.

As a matter of survival – for himself and his people – Vlad had become quite accustomed to probing others for weaknesses. If he felt that the Ottomans were in a strong position, he would play the loyal subject and allow them to march right through his lands in their quest to subdue Christians. But if he felt that the Christians to the north were getting stronger, he wouldn't hesitate to side with them and turn on his Turkish masters. In addition to all this political intrigue and maneuvering, Vlad also didn't hesitate to kill his citizens for the smallest infraction or perceived disrespect. He was a truly startling – and disturbing – figure.

Fast forward to some 400 years later. British author Bram Stoker took the frightful figure of Vlad the Impaler and imbued him with all the supernatural mystique and powers of dark Romanian folklore to create the figure of Count Dracula, which most of us are familiar with from literature, TV, and film. This book seeks to explore every single aspect of this character that did exist historically, and has been alternatively despised, lionized, fabricated, and made fodder for conspiracy theories. We leave no stone unturned as we delve into the depths of everything Dracula!

Did Dracula Really Exist?

Few others have captured the imagination in such a way as the dark, shadowy figure of Dracula. This is all, of course, thanks to the fictional narrative created by Bram Stoker in his masterpiece classic by the same name, which was first published in 1897. But there is a real person behind the hazy horror dreamed up by Bram Stoker. His name was Vlad III, a Romanian prince who ruled over the principality of Wallachia. But he was perhaps better known as *Vlad*

Tepes, which translates from the Romanian vernacular to *Vlad the Impaler*.

The raw historical data that we have on this mysterious monarch is just as frightening as any fictional horror tale. Vlad ruled with an iron fist, and as his name suggests, he wasn't at all opposed to spilling blood. Vlad was also eventually referred to by his fellow Romanians as *Drakul*, or *Dracula*, which is actually Romanian for either *dragon* or *devil*. These terms are interchangeable in the Romanian tongue.

This nickname actually stemmed from the fact that Vlad's family hailed from an inherited order of knights called the Order of the Dragon, which was akin to the Knights Templar, or similar quasi-religious military outfits of the time. The Order of the Dragon, like many Christian crusader groups before it, had been tasked with repelling the Muslim might of the Ottoman Empire. The Balkan region where we would find Vlad's Kingdom of Wallachia (modern-day Romania) had become the front lines of this holy war.

At any rate, whatever he was actually called at the time, the Romanians – and just about everyone else in a hundred-mile radius – would one day live in terrible fear of Vlad Tepes. His subjects viewed him as such a bloodthirsty tyrant that they did indeed pass down stories of Vlad drinking blood. Shortly after his death, wood carvings were made that depicted Vlad casually dining at a table surrounded by his impaled enemies, dipping his bread into their blood.

All of this, of course, fits quite nicely with the vampiric storyline we have all come to see the figure of Dracula as being a part of. As we delve deeper into the story, many truths and fictions seem to converge. But was there any truth to the superhuman connotations that Stoker later imbued this despot with? Where does the historical narrative end and the fantastical one begin? Here in this book we are going to examine the life of Vlad III, Vlad Tepes, Vlad the Impaler – Dracula, piece by piece, as the monster emerges.

The Precarious Childhood of Dracula

Most of us who have seen those old Dracula movies (or perhaps even read the classic piece of fictional literature on the subject) have assumed that it's all a work of fiction – that the trappings of the count's castle, and even the land of Transylvania, are all made up. But this is simply not the case. Bram Stoker, when he first wrote the classic vampire tale, drew upon extensive historical research. The people and places he brings forth in his narrative are not put there by accident.

Many of them did exist. There have been centuries of ever-changing borders, place names, and appellations in Eastern Europe, but at one time there really was a Romanian province called Transylvania; this is historical fact. Transylvania was a region near the Carpathian Mountains, which by the time of Dracula (or as he was otherwise known, Vlad III) had been reduced to a protectorate by the Ottoman Empire. This Islamic powerhouse had been bearing down on Eastern Europe for quite some time, and was threatening to subsume all of the Balkans.

It is said that Vlad III was most likely born sometime in the early 1430s (some sources say 1431) in Sighișoara – a then highly Germanized city in the heart of what is today Romania proper, and scholars have managed to trace down the actual house of Vlad III's birth. The building can still be visited by the curious to this very day, and it bears an inscription that testifies that this humble abode is indeed where the man forever known as Dracula was born. It is said that Vlad's father (Vlad II) worked for the Byzantine court in Constantinople, before the great metropolis's catastrophic fall to Muslim conquerors in 1453. But at the time of Vlad II's arrival in this world, his father was living in exile in Transylvania – yes, *that Transylvania* – the fabled land of vampires that first gained worldwide attention in Bram Stoker's book *Dracula*. The land that once comprised the region known as Transylvania is today a part of western Romania, spanning a breadth of over 63,000 miles. It is said that this relatively small and unassuming Eastern European kingdom served as a kind of way station on the route to Constantinople, farther east. Vlad II's father, as ruler of the realm, played an important role in defending this trade route from Turkish attacks launched from the growing threat of the Ottoman Empire.

Not much is known of Vlad's mother, except that prior to her marriage to Vlad's father she was a princess from nearby Moldovia.

Vlad II took many of his marching orders from the Holy Roman Emperor, Sigismund, the leader of the conglomerate states of Central Europe at that time. It was Emperor Sigismund who gave rise to the name of Dracula. It was under his administration that Vlad II was made a knight of the Order of the Dragon.

In 1436 Vlad Dracul was able to remove the previous Wallachian ruler, Alexandru Aldea, from power and install himself as a Wallachian prince. Just one year into his rule, however, Vlad

Dracul received the tidings that his longtime benefactor, the Holy Roman Emperor, had died. Sensing the winds of fate shifting toward the powerful Ottoman Empire, Dracul made the Machiavellian move to seek support from his former sworn enemies, and he looked for an alliance with the Turkish Sultan Murad II.

Dracul signed his new secret pact with the Turks in 1437, essentially negating his previous oath, made with the Order of the Dragon, of protecting Christendom from the Muslim advance in the Balkans. Such a move struck his Christian brethren as a direct betrayal, but Dracul knew that he would be unable to defend his realm against the mighty Ottoman state, and after the death of the Holy Roman Emperor he didn't expect aid from Central Europe to be forthcoming. Signing this alliance was the only way he had to buy time.

This maneuvering did indeed prevent the Ottomans from advancing into his realm, and instead had the Turks officially recognizing him as Prince of Wallachia. But this peace was bought with the financial price of yearly tribute having to be paid to the Ottoman Empire, and at the cost of losing the respect and trust of his former Christian allies in central Europe. This trust would be even further shattered when in 1442, Dracul, maintaining a position of neutrality, allowed the Ottoman Turks to march right through his kingdom, completely unopposed, to launch an invasion from Wallachian soil into Transylvania.

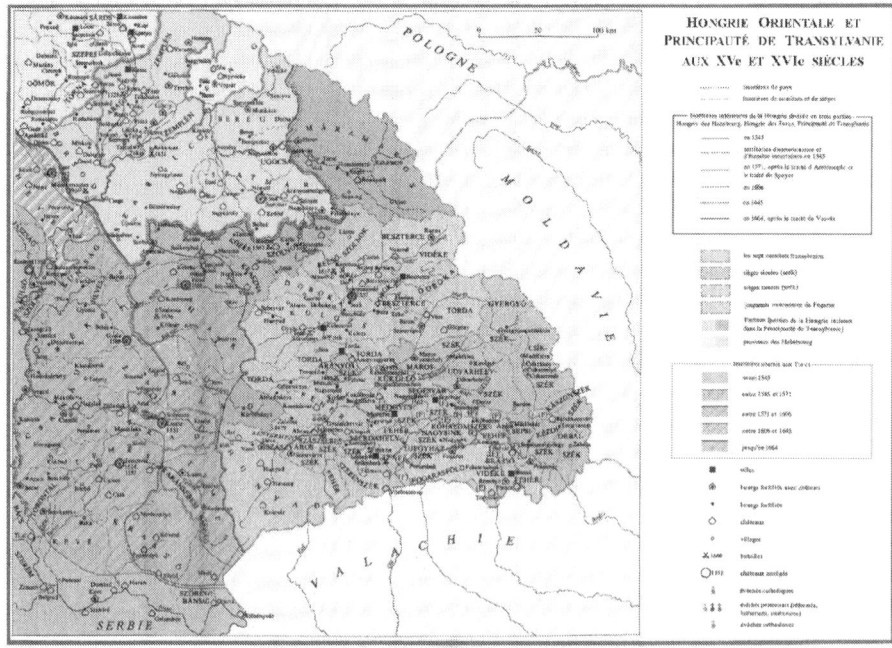

The Transylvanians put up a staunch resistance, however, and under the leadership of John Hunyadi (who was then serving as governor of the region) they were able to deal the Turks a devastating defeat. The Transylvanians, of course, hadn't taken to kindly to the fact that Dracul had let the Turks waltz through his backyard to attack them, and so immediately after repelling the Turks, John Hunyadi sent his troops into Wallachia to seize Dracul, whom they viewed as a hated Turkish collaborator.

Unlike Dracul, who had fallen back on his oaths, John Hunyadi, often called the "White Knight" of the later Crusades, was a true believer, and had dedicated his life to stop the expansion of Ottoman rule in the Balkans. With this so-called White Knight at his heels, Dracul managed to evade his pursuers and escape capture, fleeing to the protection of the Turks. His life may have been spared by seeking refuge under the sultan, but his throne would not be. In his absence, John Hunyadi had the principality of Wallachia given over to the Hungarian noble, Basarab II.

The Turks, meanwhile, gave Dracul lodging in western Turkey, where he was reasonably well cared for as a prisoner of the Ottoman Empire. But the Ottomans couldn't keep Dracul detained in their realm forever, and so, still seeking to use for him as their vassal in Wallachia, they helped him regain his throne in 1443. The Turks only gave Vlad Dracul their assistance, however, after he entered into a new agreement with them, this time not only paying an annual monetary tribute, but also sending a yearly quota of Wallachian men and boys to be conscripted into the Ottoman army.

But the darkest aspect of the deal Vlad Dracul brokered with the Turks was that he agreed to leave two of *his own sons* – Vlad III, who was just 12 years old at the time, and his younger brother Radu, just five or six – as hostages of the Ottoman state. The Ottomans wanted to hold onto Dracul's sons in order to ensure his future cooperation. It had been a long-standing tradition of the Ottomans to have their client states give them human collateral of this kind, in order to solidify their grip on subject monarch's they wished to control.

Vlad III, or as he would later become *Dracula* would remain a prisoner of the Ottomans until 1448. During his stay with the Turks he became fluent in Turkish and was taught Turkish methods of fighting, drilling with the Ottoman military. From the outset, the boys were treated fairly well, but even so, one can only imagine how terrifying the ordeal would have been. Just imagine these two scared children ripped from the protection of their parents and placed in a foreign land they knew nothing about, with strangers who, even if they espoused politeness, were mostly ambivalent about their long-term welfare.

And Vlad, the older of the two, would have understood the situation much more clearly than Radu, realizing that their very lives depended on their father's cooperation with the sultan.

Many scholars have noted that this heavy realization at such a young and impressionable age must have had a major impact on the psychology of Vlad III. They have pointed out that the understanding that his life could be so easily lost may have given Vlad III a lasting mindset that life was cheap, and people – including a father's own sons – were easily expendable.

It is quite rational to speculate that it was this devastating experience as a hostage of the Turks that shaped the mentality of the man who would become the cruel, cold, and callous *Vlad the Impaler*. Vlad III's younger brother was no doubt shielded from much of this bleak psychological baggage because he was little at the time, simply too young to process much of what was happening around him.

But perhaps he wasn't completely unaffected, being subject to some of the more egregious predation of the harem culture of the sultan's court. Radu would later acquire the nickname *Radu the Handsome*, and was said to have had beautiful features. Unfortunately for him, it was these good looks that got him the unwanted attention of Sultan Murad's son, Mehmed, who began to pursue the youth for his own pleasure. According to one disturbing account from the Greek historian Laonikos Chalkokondyles, Mehmed called young Radu into his chambers on at least one occasion in an attempt to seduce him.

With Radu secluded with him in his room, Mehmed allegedly began to passionately kiss the boy, but Radu is said to have hidden a knife on his person, and stabbing the sultan's son in the thigh, managed to escape. The account then goes on to state that Radu climbed up a tree in the courtyard and remained there until Mehmed, bandaged up by his physician, limped away from the scene. Besides this one shocking description of the blatant predation of Radu by way of Mehmed, most sources state that

Vlad and Radu were treated humanely during the first year of their captivity.

But in 1444, when war broke out between Hungary and the Ottoman Empire, the courtesy of their captors began to change. Things especially came to a head when Dracul, stuck between two competing oaths, came under pressure to come back to the side of his Christian brethren of central and eastern Europe. You see, even though he had sworn allegiance to the Turks, he was still bound by the oath he had taken on behalf of the Order of the Dragon. Despite the danger posed to his captive children, Dracul was eventually persuaded to take up the oath he had made, all those years ago, to the Order of the Dragon.

Dracul certainly didn't take this decision lightly, and before making it, he wrote a letter to the crusading Christian authorities stating his dilemma. He said, "Please understand that I have allowed my little children to be butchered for the sake of the Christian peace." By joining the other Christian crusaders in the fight against the Islamic advance, Dracul fully believed that he had just signed the death warrant for his captive sons.

But the Turks did not execute his children after all. Although their treatment had become a little bit harsher for their father's betrayal to the Ottoman State, it had been determined that the hostages would serve the sultan better alive as bargaining chips, than they would as dead corpses in the ground. So, it was determined that Vlad "Dracula" Tepes and his brother Radu the Handsome would live to see another day.

Dracula and the Tightrope of Leadership

It is said that during his long captivity, Dracul's son Vlad III grew increasingly cynical and cold to the world around him. He was the hostage of a hostile country, and he knew that his life could be snuffed out at any time. For him, life had been forever stained with a certain sense of cheapness that he couldn't shake from his psyche. This jaded view of humanity would stay with Dracula for the rest of his life. Meanwhile, after international tensions had briefly cooled, the Ottomans established communication with their wayward former ally Vlad Dracul, and let him know that the sons he had left in their care were indeed still alive.

The Turks then offered to enter into a new agreement with the Wallachian monarch, which was then signed and ratified in 1447. According to these new rules of engagement, Vlad Dracul now had to not only adhere to all of the terms of the previous agreement, he also had to deport 4000 Bulgarian refugees (who had fled Bulgaria from previous Ottoman incursions) out of Wallachia. Vlad Dracul had to have known that by shipping these beleaguered Bulgarians back to Ottoman-controlled Bulgaria he was exposing them to either certain death or enslavement at the hands of the Turks.

When Dracul's arch nemesis John Hunyadi got wind of this latest betrayal, it was too much for him to bear. In November 1447 he sent an invasion force into Wallachia to take out Dracul once and for all. After a brief siege, Dracul's forces were defeated. As his last lines of defense were being obliterated, Dracul himself rode off on a perilous course, seeking escape from his adversaries. But the long arm of Hunyadi would soon catch up with him, and in the vast marshes on the outskirts of Bucharest, Dracul was caught and slaughtered.

Hunyadi then returned to Dracul's former Wallachian dominion in triumph, declaring himself to be the prince of Wallachia. This euphoric proclamation would not be officially put into practice, however, and Hunyadi would install Basarab II's brother, Vladislav II, to the Wallachian throne instead. Upon hearing the news of Dracul's demise, the Ottoman sultan summoned the slain leader's children Radu and Vlad Dracula to debrief them on the events and to grant them their freedom. This showed a surprising degree of kindness and compassion on the sultan's part, and for the most part he treated Dracul's sons as though they were the children of a high-ranking slain Ottoman official.

After his father's defeat, Vlad Dracula, the "son of the dragon" himself, was given an official post as officer in the Ottoman army. He was instructed to bide his time until the moment was ripe to take back the Wallachian throne, for himself and ostensibly for the Ottomans, to make Wallachia once again serve Turkish interests as a vassal state. The moment of opportunity they were waiting for came in 1448, when war broke out in Kosovo between Kosovars and Vladislav II.

The Hungarian contingent led by Vladislav II was ultimately defeated, and it was while Vladislav II was bogged down in the trenches of Kosovo that Dracula made his move. With the aid of Ottoman troops, he seized control of Wallachia. This first brief reign wouldn't last long, however, before Vladislav II rallied enough troops to come marching right back to Wallachia and remove the usurping Dracula from power. Dracula then fled back to Ottoman territory in 1448, ending his first attempt at Wallachian rule after less than two months.

Here he lingered for a short time before heading to Suceava, the capital of Moldova, where he placed himself at the mercy of his uncle Bogdan II and other Moldovan relatives in the region. Dracula would remain in the embrace of his Moldovan family members until Bogdan II was assassinated in 1451. Dracula was then sent running once again, this time to that place of vampiric legend, Transylvania, where he sought the aid of none other than his father's own killer; John Hunyadi.

Being forced to seek help from the man who'd had his father killed must have made Vlad Dracula's already contemptuous outlook on life even more cynical. Hunyadi's own tolerance of Dracula was tepid at best, and his true intentions were revealed in a letter dated February 6th, 1452, in which he gave local authorities, in regard to Dracula, the following instruction, "It is better that you capture him and chase him out of the country." It was shortly after this proclamation was made that Dracula reluctantly returned to Moldovia.

And it was here, on May 29th, 1453, that Dracula would hear the news that had shocked the Christian world; Constantinople – the greatest bulwark of Christianity in the East –had fallen. Two years later, Dracula once again sought permission from Hunyadi to find a permanent home for himself in Transylvania, and this time Hunyadi (surprisingly) obliged. One of the factors in this sudden acceptance of Dracula was apparently due to a rapidly deteriorating relationship with Vladislav II.

Hunyadi had apparently seized several duchies just outside of Wallachia, angering the ruler and creating a schism between them. After accepting Dracula under his auspices in Transylvania, Hunyadi then began to make a complete reversal on his former disdain of the man, and finally came over to his side, deciding that he would be the best suited to rule Wallachia after all. This was one of the last decisions that Hunyadi would make before he died of a protracted illness somewhere near Belgrade on the 11th of August, 1456.

It was shortly after hearing the news of this legendary Transylvanian ruler's demise that Dracula decided to make his move. He gathered a contingent of Wallachian fighters from his most ardent supporters. They marched through the Transylvanian mountains and out onto the Wallachian plain, where he and his men faced off against the army of Vladislav II. This was an absolutely pivotal moment in Dracula's life – even the stars themselves seemed to speak of the momentous occasion.

It is said that Haley's Comet, a celestial body that has long been associated with momentous events, was in the sky that night as Dracula's army collided with his rival, Vladislav II's, forces. Before the night was over, Vladislav's army was ultimately defeated, and Vladislav himself was sent running for his life. He was eventually rounded up and executed on August 20th, clearing the way for Dracula to install himself as the undisputed ruler of Wallachia once again.

But he was a ruler with some fairly twisted and tangled allegiances from the very outset of his reign. On September 6th, 1456 he had sworn an oath of loyalty to the central European stronghold of Hungary, but then just a few days thereafter he went directly to the Hungarian's most bitter enemy, the Ottoman Turks, and swore his fealty to them as well. Vlad Dracula's friendship with two sides of an incredibly bitter Balkan conflict was just the beginning of his journey through all the twists and turns of the tortuously tangled tightrope he was walking.

Dracula Takes Back His Throne

When Vlad Dracula arrived back in Tirgoviste, the capital of Wallachia, he found his kingdom literally in ruins. The former royal castle was left in rubble from constant warfare, and repeated attacks from Turkish and Hungarian armies alike. Growing weary of not having his own impregnable fortress, by 1459 Dracula had decided that the ruins must be rebuilt. And employing the crude and sadistic cunning that would later make him so famous, he devised a sadistic plot to get his new "Castle Dracula" off the drawing board and into physical existence.

In order to do this as expediently as possible, the cold, calculating Dracula decided to use the *boyars*, the nobility of Wallachia, as slave labor to build his new palace. Dracula had already held a deep contempt for the rich nobility who had long sided with his ousted rival Vladislav II, and in early 1459 he found even more reason to stoke the fires of his hatred against them.

It was apparently shortly after the New Year's festivities had subsided that Dracula learned the truth about what had happened to his older brother Mircea, who had died under the direction of Vladislav II. Dracula learned that the nobility had demanded that his brother be buried alive. Seeking to confirm the atrocity before he carried out his own vengeance, Dracula had his minions search for the gravesite of his slain brother and had the body exhumed. Upon digging up his brother's corpse, just as he had been informed was the case, he found him buried face down, still fixed in a gruesome pose of terror, as if he were attempting to dig himself out.

Now feeling he had justice on his side (no matter how broadly he defined the word *justice*) Vlad Dracula had a large portion of the nobility rounded up and forced to work on his new castle. It is said that he had the terrified nobles form a human chain up and down the mountain passes, and they carried and passed from hand to hand the heavy stones and other building materials needed at the construction site. Dracula is said to have stood over them with a whip, lashing out against this human chain of slave labor if he deemed any one of them to be working too slowly.

Many of these poor, hapless souls were worked to death in the process, and others simply tripped and fell to their death as they attempted to carry large stones up the mountainside. Those who survived the construction of Dracula's castle did not meet a much better fate after its successful completion – it is said that after subsequent purges many of them simply disappeared from the record after 1459.

In order to fill the positions that were left open after the massacre of the original nobility, Dracula reached out to the peasant class. He offered them the land and wealth of the dead nobles, as long as they swore an oath of loyalty to him. For most of the downtrodden poor, it was an offer they couldn't refuse. This was a fairly brilliant tactic on the part of Dracula, in which he sought to raise up the peasant class to the nobility, with their newfound fortune directly tied to him.

This was how Dracula attempted to destroy the old nobility that had betrayed him and his family in the past, and then at the same time raise up a new class of Wallachians, a new nobility, which would be completely loyal to him.

Surviving records from this time period reveal that there is an astonishing truth in the legends of these purges. A comparison of the names listed on the local council from 1456 to 1462, about 90% of the entries are new.

But it wasn't only the noble class at whom Dracula would direct his ire. Regardless of place or station, anyone who besmirched his sense of justice and ethics became a target of his rage. In one notable instance Dracula is said to have happened across a peasant man with some rather ragged clothing, and became peculiarly disturbed by his apparel.

The man's disheveled attire enraged Dracula to such an extent that he approached the man and inquired into his home life, asking him, "Your wife is assuredly of the kind who remains idle. How is it possible that your shirt does not cover the calf of your leg?" Before the startled man could respond, Dracula forcefully continued, "She is not worthy of living in my realm. May she perish!" Dracula apparently (like many men of his time period) placed all responsibility for a man's home and hearth on the shoulders of the woman, and he deemed that this man's ragged garments indicated a slothful wife who refused to properly repair them.

Fair judgement or not, Dracula was so perturbed by the very thought of this that he immediately called for the poor woman's execution. In fact, even while the man in question was in attendance, Vlad Dracula had his wife summoned before him and summarily killed. But even though the man no doubt must have cried out in anguish at the impalement of his wife, Dracula, with his warped sense of justice, believed he was doing the man a favor. And further attempting to be equitable in the exchange, immediately after the wife's death, he brought forth another woman from his court whom he deemed would serve as an excellent replacement for the man's first wife!

This newly requisitioned bride is said to have also borne witness to the first wife's execution. As the story goes, consequently the new wife worked so hard she had no time to eat!

Dracula apparently wanted to be deeply involved in all aspects of his subjects' lives, truly thinking that he knew what was best for them. Because he was so interfering, Dracula soon established a kind of puritanical rule through sheer terror, all throughout his realm.

In Vlad Dracula's dictatorship, no matter was too far removed to not be of his concern. If, for example, it was called to his attention that there had been instances of extramarital affairs in his realm, it wasn't uncommon for Dracula to see to it that the offenders had their sexual organs cut off.

As well as prying into the personal lives of his subjects on an individual level, Dracula also was known to mete out wholesale punishments for isolated, individual offenses. On many occasions, if one member of a village committed a crime against the state, Dracula would condemn the whole enclave for that one individual's crimes. Whether it was murder or thievery – no matter how great or petty – Dracula would sometimes punish the entire community the criminal came from so as to teach the rest of his neighbors a lesson. This was Vlad Dracula's harsh sense of justice. It was due to these austere measures that Dracula managed to terrify his subjects into perfect, peaceful submission to his iron rule.

As a result of these austere measures, it was said that crime quickly became nonexistent under Dracula's rule, and families could leave all of their doors unlocked and their valuables right in the front yard. The fear of reprisal was so great that no one dared to steal so much as one gold coin in the realm of Dracula! Lending credence to this legend is the tale of the golden cup. Dracula supposedly placed one of his priceless golden cups in front of a fountain in the public square of the capital, and then left it there unguarded, as if he were practically daring a thief to come along and grab it. According to the legend, no thief ever dared so much as touch the cup!!

If Vlad felt that he could not control the behavior of certain members of his populace, he wanted to eliminate them. This was evidenced in the telling of how he chose to tackle a panhandling problem that his capital was facing. He declared a massive banquet at his palace and invited all of the local beggars and vagabonds to attend. After these poor downtrodden souls had their fill, Dracula himself then made an appearance and asked them if they would like to be free from all of their burdens, cares, concerns, and worries in life.

The merry group, wondering what happy reward was waiting for them next, cheered that they would. Dracula then stepped out of the building, and had all of the doors and windows of the banquet hall boarded up before ordering the entire building to be burned down. His method of "freeing" the panhandlers of their burdens was to burn them alive. It was a strange and terrible kind of peace to live in the protective embrace of Vlad Dracula

Beating the Drums of War

Up until late 1456, Dracula had been a duplicitous leader in the eyes of Christian Europe. Because he had originally been installed by the Ottoman Empire, it was felt that his loyalties still lay with the Ottoman Turks and not with Christendom. And after the death of the de facto leader of the central European crusaders, the "White Knight" John Hunyadi, his son and successor Ladislaus Hunyadi became one of Dracula's main detractors.

From his official posting as the captain general of Hungary, Ladislaus Hunyadi never ceased in his disparagement and criticisms of the "son of the dragon," Vlad Dracula. He even went so far to rattle off a letter to the King of Hungary, declaring that Dracula had no intention of remaining faithful to the cause of Christian Europe. In this missive he also went on to urge Hungarian nobility to support the slain Vladislav II's brother, Dan III, in a campaign to reclaim the throne of Wallachia from Dracula.

This maneuvering to support his hated rival was of course an unpardonable sin in Dracula's book. And it really should come as no surprise that Vlad Dracula didn't shed a tear when he heard of his antagonist Ladislaus Hunyadi's execution on grounds of suspected treason to the Hungarian throne on March 16th, 1457. Dracula couldn't have failed to see the immense irony that his rival, who so often accused him of treachery, found himself executed on the very same charge.

This bit of luck against his nemesis then proved to bear even more fruit for Vlad Dracula. He soon received tidings that in the wake of Hunyadi's demise, discord was growing in Hungary. Ladislaus Hunyadi's mother, Erzebet, had gathered factions loyal to her slain son, which were led by her brother, Michael Szilagyi, who was a Hungarian regent and general, and managed to provoke a civil war in Hungary.

Taking advantage of the chaos, Vlad Dracula aided his cousin Stephen (son of his Uncle Bogdan II) in seizing Moldova in June of 1457. He turned his troops on Transylvania, where he led a lightning raid that led to looting and pillaging in Transylvanian towns such as Brasov, Sibiu, and others, on a massive scale. Stories later circulated among the German principalities that spoke of the horror that Vlad Dracula employed during his punitive strikes against the Transylvanians. Tales recalled the way Dracula seized hundreds of men, women, and children from their villages, and took them all the way back to Wallachia, where he had them promptly impaled.

The prisoners no doubt figured they were in for a life of servitude as slaves; they had no idea that they were simply being transferred to his realm so he could amuse himself with their demise at a leisurely pace. Incredibly, Vlad Dracula expended valuable time and resources just to be able to carry out this protracted torture of the Transylvanian citizenry. But these bizarre acts of cruelty were just the beginning of his growing legacy as *Vlad the Impaler*.

Meanwhile, as the hostilities between the warring factions came to a close, Dracula inserted himself into the peace talks between the two parties. Adding to the already rich layers in this tapestry of irony, Vlad aligned himself on the side of Michael Szilagyi, the uncle of his dead antagonist, Ladislaus Hunyadi. They entered into an agreement to place Ladislaus Hunyadi's little brother, Mathias Corvinus, on the Hungarian throne on January 24th, 1458.

Dracula then went on to forge a treaty in which he not only pledged his military cooperation, but also made an economic commitment. He promised to allow Hungarian merchants to have free reign in Wallachia, allowing them to buy and sell merchandise without any extra taxation or fees. Dracula would go back on his promise to these merchants, however, when towards the end of that very same year, in the winter of 1458, he decided to place high tariffs on all Transylvanian goods coming into his kingdom.

This sparked what could be called a Balkan trade war, which soon led into an all-out war between Hungary and the forces of Vlad Dracula that would wax and wane for the next two years. During this conflict Dracula would commit one of his worst atrocities, when in 1459 he seized some 400 Transylvanians who had been living in his realm and had them all locked in a room before setting the building on fire and burning them all alive. From here, Dracula continued his bloody reign of terror, slaughtering whole towns.

In July of 1460 Dracula seized the Transylvanian fief of Fagaras. Here he rounded up all of the town's citizenry, men, women, and children, and had them all impaled, leaving their dead bodies held aloft for all to see.

But these conflicts with his Balkan neighbors would prove to be just the opening acts. The main event would come when Vlad Dracula declared war on the Ottoman Empire.

According to the Turkish account of how this war broke out, it all began when Dracula decided that he didn't need to pay the annual tribute that he had been sending the Ottomans for years. According to some reports, Dracula had been exhibiting outright defiance toward the Turks on these matters as early as 1456, before the trade war in the Balkans had broken out. In a letter dated September 19th, 1456, Dracula was found describing measures of outright defiance he had taken against the Ottomans.

In this missive, Dracula claimed to have detained Turkish envoys who were sent by the sultan to demand tribute from him, and proceeded to request a Hungarian contingent of at least 50 chosen men to be sent to bolster his forces in case the Turks attempted any further aggression. What Dracula apparently failed to mention about this Turkish envoy that he held in custody was that in a fit of rage he had cruelly nailed their customary turban headgear to their skulls…

The account of what transpired was later reported by Russian sources, who described the sequence of events. "At one time, some envoys from the Turkish sultan came to him. When they came and they bowed to him according to their custom, they did not take their turbans off. Vlad Dracula, who was apparently offended that the men did not remove their apparel before seeking audience with him, asked, 'Why do you do this towards a great ruler?' To which they answered, 'This is our custom.' "

Vlad Dracula then replied, "I too wish to strengthen your law so that you may be firm." Dracula then apparently directed his troops to use small metal spikes to permanently hammer the turbans onto the men's heads. As the Turkish men were left screaming on the floor with pools of blood flowing from their punctured skulls, Dracula then promptly informed them, "[Now] go and tell your master that he is *accustomed* to endure such shame from you, but we are not [so] *accustomed*."

If this story is true – and the fact that there are at least two documented sources, both Dracula himself, and the later Russian chroniclers, tends to give it at least a small measure of credibility – it would seem to indicate that the Ottoman sultan demonstrated extreme patience with the Wallachian ruler. If the sultan did not care too much for Dracula, he would have sent an immediate invasion force to remove him from power after suffering such an outrage.

But the fact that Dracula was able to get away with such an outrageous offense just goes to show how complicated the relationship between Vlad Dracula and Sultan Mehmed really was. The two had known each other since childhood, with Vlad growing up side by side with the future sultan, while he was a hostage at the court of Mehmed's father. The two seemed to understand each other, and even if they didn't always like the other, they both seemed to have a profound respect for their counterpart.

And Vlad's abuse of the sultan's courtiers because he felt disrespected appears to be something the sultan understood and was ready to accept. At any rate, Dracula bragged about this incident in a letter to the Hungarian king in 1456, hoping to entice him to sending a Hungarian contingent. These efforts however, would fall flat. For whatever reason, the Hungarian king refused to send any troops.

Some point to this fact as part of the reason why the embittered Vlad began to stir up trouble in Transylvania. According to this theory, this is why he suddenly raised tariffs with previously friendly trading partners, and then launched his subsequent military raids on peaceful Transylvanian communities. Vlad, whose realm was situated between the great power of Hungary to the north, and the even greater power of the Ottoman Empire the south, always found himself forced to play to both.

If one side didn't seem to be rendering any immediate benefit to him, he would then maneuver to the other. This explains how Vlad could ask for aid from Hungary one moment and then attack its holdings in Transylvania in reprisal shortly thereafter. And so it was just as he was easing the hostilities that he had brought forth with his northern neighbors that the Ottomans in the south came to tighten their grip on him once again. These matters came to a head when the Ottoman Sultan Mehmed II sent an envoy led by the Greek dignitary Thomas Katabolinos, demanding that Vlad personally report to the sultan in order to explain his insolence.

Dracula, of course, knew that meeting the sultan would only mean certain death, so instead of complying with the wishes of the envoy, he had them all promptly executed. Without even officially declaring war, Vlad Dracula went on the offensive against the entire Ottoman Empire. Taking just a small contingent of his army with him, he then approached the nearest Turkish outpost of his territory in Giurgiu, a fortress his father Dracul had founded, but which had fallen to the Turks in 1444.

Here, using the full extent of the cunning mind at his command, Dracula (who had learned fluent Turkish during his childhood captivity), came up with a ploy to take control of the fort without a fight. He simply rode out to the gates of the fortress and confidently shouted out orders in Turkish for the guards to let him in. The guards, apparently not accustomed to hearing their native tongue in the Balkans, believed that the orders must be from a legitimate source, and opened the gates to the fort.

Once inside, Dracula and his men revealed their true character and began to engage in a wholesale slaughter of the Turks. Dracula then set up a permanent base in Giurgiu and used it as a launching pad for the beginning of his invasion of the Ottoman Empire as a whole. Vlad wanted the Ottomans to know that he had declared war on them, and he wanted them to know it in the harshest of terms.

The nearby Danube river had frozen into solid ice, and was easily traversable by Dracula's forces, allowing them to cross into Ottoman-held Bulgaria, looting, burning, and pillaging with virtual impunity before crossing back over to safety on the other side. Dracula is said to have killed thousands during these lightning raids. The fear that he instilled on these campaigns was such as Ottoman commanders had never experienced before, with massive casualties, and fear mounting.

Dracula himself attempted to tally up and document the death count in February, 1462, when he sent a personal letter to the Hungarian king, in which he is often said to have unabashedly reported, "I have killed men and women, old and young, who lived at Oblucitza and Novoselo, where the Danube flows into the sea, up to Rahova, which is located near Chilia, from the lower Danube up to such places as Samovit and Ghighen. We killed 23,884 Turk and Bulgars without counting those whom we burned in homes or whose heads were not cut by our soldiers. Thus, your highness must know that I have broken the peace with him." (Sultan Mehmed II)

And then as a follow-up to this letter, Dracula had a personal package delivered to the king of Hungary, in the form of two large bags which were filled with the decapitated heads, and cut off ears and noses, of Turks and Bulgars, that he and his men had severed from their enemies. Along with this grisly proof of his brutality, Vlad Dracula also sought to use his slain enemies as personal ornaments in his capital of Tirgoviste, forcing over 1000 Ottoman troops to march north to the city, where he had them all impaled just outside of his palace.

Creating a veritable forest of dead, impaled Turks, Dracula was sending a dire message to the Ottomans that they would not be able to ignore. The Turks soon responded to this horrific testament by sending a group of 18,000 men to capture a strategic Wallachian port on the Danube river called Brila. Once gaining this strategic foothold, Sultan Mehmed II used it as his own launching point to stage attacks against villages in Wallachia.

It was during one of these expeditions that Vlad Dracula managed to get behind one of the raiding parties the Turks had sent out, and catching them by complete surprise, tore into the Turkish contingent. In the ensuing onslaught Dracula's army is said to have killed 10,000 Ottoman troops. This staggering defeat led Mehmed II to personally head his army, in an effort to boost morale in the next major assault waged against Dracula, in May of 1462.

Vlad had destroyed many of the port cities along the Danube, but this was only a minor setback for the large army that Mehmed had prepared, and by the end of May, a massive force of nearly 100,000 troops packing 120 cannons came on a direct crash course from Constantinople, all the way to Wallachia. Most sovereigns in Vlad Dracula's position would have been wracked with worry, but as the drums of war grew louder, Vlad Dracula wasn't missing a beat.

The Dragon's Crusade

As the war machine of the Ottomans slowly made its way to Wallachia, Vlad Dracula asked for additional support from Christian Europe. The pope was undoubtedly impressed by the valor and initiative of Vlad Dracula, but his hands were already tied, and the call for a new crusade would not be taken up by anyone outside of Wallachia. Vlad Dracula and his small army were, for the time being, on their own against a foe that outnumbered them at least three to one.

Vlad Dracula sought to augment his numbers by issuing a general draft and call to arms among the peasantry. This pulled about 30,000 additional troops of all ages into his total fighting force. Dracula's secret weapon, however, was his "war wagons." In what was the Wallachian version of a modern tank, steel wagons, which were basically mobile fortresses, were chained together and equipped with artillery. These wagons would prove to be quite formidable, as they provided a platform from which arrows and artillery could bombard the Turks with virtual impunity.

As the Ottomans neared his realm, Dracula had patrols of troops marching up and down the frontiers of Wallachia, keeping track of the enemy's progress. It was noted that most of the Ottoman army was being sent up the Danube River, in order to reach Tirgoviste by way of the rivers. But as soon as the Turks attempted to step off the river banks, a Wallachian contingent emerged from the wilderness and waylaid them with such intensive arrow and artillery fire that they were forced to pull back.

But in June of 1462 the Turks finally made landfall near the Wallachian village of Turnu. It was here that Vlad Dracula first deployed his war wagons, and it is said that 300 Ottoman troops were killed under withering fire in the first few moments of the Ottoman landing, nearly pushing the Turks back to the river once again. But the Ottomans held out, and more importantly, they were able to position their own artillery and use a system of 120 cannons to blast the Wallachians back into the woodlands from which they had emerged.

It was after this initial victory that the sultan revealed an ace up his sleeve: Vlad Dracula's own brother, Radu. The younger brother of Vlad Dracula had never left the auspices of the Ottomans, and since Vlad Dracula's fall from the sultan's grace he had been groomed to be a potential replacement. The Ottomans fully intended to capture Dracula, kill him, and replace him with his younger brother. Radu was even given charge of his own military unit consisting of 4000 men on horseback.

With the Ottoman army heading ever closer to his capital, Vlad decided to resort to a scorched earth policy and began to burn all the vegetation behind him. He even polluted all the wells, so that food and water would be scarce for the weary Turks. Dracula also sought to make the terrain as difficult to traverse as possible by having his engineers dam up tributaries and cause the open plains to be flooded, creating vast marshlands to slow down the progress of the Turkish advance.

This natural barrier was also augmented by booby traps that had been set up all throughout the forest region of southern Wallachia, including hidden trap doors that led to a sudden fall and – you guessed it – certain impalement on the spikes hidden below. Along with these traps, Dracula had sentries who were always on the lookout, shadowing the movements of the Ottoman troops, and the second any of them took a wrong turn or wandered away from the main contingent, they were there to spring upon them and kill them before they could escape back to their encampment.

All these factors served to slowly whittle away at the sultan's army before he even engaged Dracula's army in open combat. Along with altering the environment, creating booby traps and using hit-and-run tactics, one other irregular method of warfare that Dracula is rumored to have used is the tactic of sending diseased members of his own troops (most likely infected with the bubonic plague) to secretly infiltrate the Ottoman camp for the sole purpose of spreading the disease!

It was under this severe duress that the Ottoman army slowly made its progress toward Vlad Dracula's castle. Only after passing through much difficulty did they reach the mountain passes just outside Tirgoviste. And it was here that they first beheld the shocking sight of Dracula's *forest of the impaled*, a veritable forest of spikes with thousands of dead Turks impaled upon them.

Just as this shock settled into their consciousness, Vlad decided to strike. In particular, he wanted to deliver the Turks a killing blow by capturing and killing the sultan. He believed that if he decapitated the Ottoman army, it would quickly disintegrate into chaos and he would be the victor. It was this desired objective that led Vlad Dracula to launch what would become known as his "Night Attack" against the Ottomans.

For this attack he couldn't rely upon the motley crew of peasant infantry he had cobbled together for previous skirmishes; instead he used only his best troops. He gathered together about 10,000 experienced and formidable fighters and sent them out to strike the sultan in the darkness of night, on June 17th, 1462. In true vampiric fashion the battle would last from sunset until just before the sun came up, with Dracula and his minions leaving countless dead in their wake.

Similar to the way he had tricked sentries at the fort in Giurgiu, Dracula is said to have used Turkish prisoners to gain access to the camp through subterfuge before having the camp guards killed and the main army rush through, letting loose on the sleeping army with steel blades and arrows. It is also claimed that Dracula had spies on the ground relaying important intelligence as to the location of guard posts and important tents within the encampment.

Further legends even claim that immediately before the attack was launched, Dracula had disguised himself as a Turk and walked right into the encampment, his enemies unaware. It is this image in particular, of Dracula walking quietly among his enemies, unnoticed and unacknowledged, that has given rise to some of the more fantastical depictions in film and literature that has imbued Dracula with the supernatural power of invisibility.

Dracula is often depicted as being able to change his form and become a shadow on the walls of his enemies if necessary, in order to gather intimate intelligence about them. Supernatural powers or not, the sleeping Ottomans were taken completely off guard by the intrusion, and woke up to swords being stabbed into their chests and arrowheads piercing their skulls.

Although some say that Vlad aspired to be the next crusading "White Knight," picking up the mantle from the deceased John Hunyadi, his tactics were certainly not of the noble caliber of his predecessor. Vlad Dracula was using every underhanded trick in the book in order to defeat his enemy. For Vlad a win was a win, no matter how it may have been achieved. Even if he had to resort to slaughtering his enemy while they slept, for Vlad the victory would be no less legitimate. Vlad was a survivor, after all, and he had learned during his harsh life to use every method at his disposal to ensure that his survival continued. His butchering of Turks while they slept was just a function of this pragmatic strategy.

And in reality, if Vlad had pitted his forces against the Turks head on in open battle his outnumbered army would probably have been annihilated in short order. Under the bleak conditions that existed for the Wallachians, it was only someone as crafty and cruelly cunning as Dracula who could utilize such incredible feats of subterfuge to pull off an impossible victory. And this is precisely what Dracula sought when he tried to catch the Turkish encampment off guard and slay their leader, the sultan, as he slept.

But when they came upon a large, extravagant tent they believed to be the sultan's, they were disappointed to find that it was not the lodging of Mehmed, but rather the tent of a couple of lower ranking officials who were traveling with him. These men were quickly put to the sword regardless, as Vlad Dracula's cold, cruel eyes sought out the real prize, Sultan Mehmed himself. But by the time Dracula finally located his tent it had been surrounded by his crack troops, who put up such a ferocious defense that none of the Wallachians could get near it.

After intense fighting, in which Dracula himself was wounded, the Wallachians were forced to retreat – but not before inflicting some serious losses on their foe, killing as many as 15,000 Turks. It is said that this devastating attack was nearly enough to make the sultan consider a retreat right then and there, but after discussions with his advisors he determined to soldier on. The Ottoman army then finally found their way to the very gates of Dracula's palace, but to their surprise it was already abandoned, the gates wide open, and only a courtyard full of thousands of impaled bodies there to greet the Turkish would-be conquerors.

With the sultan's superstitious men thoroughly spooked, Dracula and company nowhere to be seen, and no real gains to be had in occupying such a haunted piece of terrain, the Ottoman sultan decided to make a strategic retreat. The Ottomans seemed to have been chasing nothing but ghouls and ghosts during their Wallachian campaign, and they were left with nothing much more than nightmares to take with them. Before making a full withdrawal, however, the sultan did leave one final parting gift for Vlad Dracula – the permanent installation of his brother Radu in southern Wallachia.

Vlad Dracula's Escape

Even though Vlad Dracula technically scored a victory against the Ottomans and managed to repel them back to Turkey, as 1462 came to a close he found his own grip on power hanging by the most tenuous of threads. His resistance against the Turks was an extremely costly one, and since he had ordered the destruction of almost all of the natural resources of the land, his own people were suffering as a consequence. Furthermore, many of his most loyal troops had been killed in the conflict, leaving Vlad Dracula dangerously bereft of supporters after the end of hostilities.

When he sensed that the walls were closing in on him, Vlad Dracula engineered his escape from his own kingdom. He'd built a secret passage, and it became quite useful in this moment of desperation, as he used it to sneak out of his castle and on through the mountains to Transylvania. There is a Transylvanian legend of just how this escape is alleged to have transpired. According to the tale, a Turkish contingent led by Dracula's brother Radu was closing in on Dracula's fortress stronghold, reaching the "hill of Poenari" just on the other side of the Arges River, from which Dracula's castle could be clearly seen.

According to the legend, one of Dracula's relatives happened to be part of the Turk's slave army of Janissaries (elite infantry units). Wishing to send his relative a warning that the Turks would soon have him surrounded, this relative is said to have stood atop the hill late one evening, and placed a note with his scribbled warning affixed upon an arrowhead. He then aimed toward the light that could be seen from one of the castle windows, and managed to launch the arrow into Castle Dracula. The legend then goes on to state that it was Vlad's Transylvanian wife (of whom there seems to be no record) who found the letter, and upon reading it, realized the imminent danger they were in.

Apparently giving up on ever finding a way out of the predicament, the story goes that Dracula's wife then strode atop the battlements of the castle and declared to him that she would, "rather have her body rot and be eaten by the fish of the Arges [River] than be led into captivity by the Turks." She is then alleged to have jumped off the ramparts of the castle, falling to her death in the river below. As far-fetched as this whole account may seem, lending credence to the story is the fact that the section of the river into which Dracula's wife is said to have fallen is, to this very day, referred to by the local citizenry as the "Princess's River."

But whether or not there was such a dramatic scene just prior to his escape, as soon as Dracula performed his disappearing act his brother Radu, who had been patiently waiting for just such a moment, was proclaimed as the new prince and installed in his place on the Wallachian throne. Vlad's brother Radu was much more palatable for the Turks and he fully intended to replace his brother outright. Vlad, meanwhile, knowing that he could not return to Wallachia and remain alive, sought aid elsewhere. Vlad Dracula met with the king of Hungary, Mathias Corvinus, in November of that year, in the town hall of Brasov, in the Transylvanian Alps.

By the time Dracula met up with his potential benefactor King Mathias, his brother Radu was already making major inroads in southern Transylvania, promising the same merchants that Dracula had instigated a trade war with a return to economic normalcy, and fair compensation for their losses. This led the city authorities of the trading center of Brasov to unilaterally decide to throw in their lot with Radu, recognizing him as the rightful prince of Wallachia. As this important city was one of the main generators of revenue in his kingdom, King Mathias felt that he had no choice but to follow suit.

And shortly after his meeting with Vlad Dracula he made it official, and he too recognized Prince Radu III as the sovereign of Wallachia. Vlad Dracula was now essentially a king without a kingdom. Despite his decision to not recognize Vlad Dracula's sovereignty, King Mathias at first pledged to offer Vlad support in the form of an imperial guard and a place of safe haven in his realm. But even these overtures would be cancelled when Dracula was abruptly arrested by the Hungarian authorities on November 26th, 1462.

Rather than being rewarded for his bravery and valor against the Hungarians' sworn enemy, Vlad was placed under immediate house arrest and his brother Radu was recognized as the legitimate ruler of Wallachia. Radu officially moved into the Wallachian capital – forest of impaled corpses and all – shortly thereafter. Vlad Dracula would remain a prisoner of the Hungarian throne for the next 12 years. Not much is known about his years of captivity.

There is even some argument as to where he was held. Some point to Solomon's Tower, the traditional home for political prisoners in Hungary. Others maintain that there is no record of Dracula being imprisoned there, and it seems much more likely to them that he was simply held under guard at the king's palace, subjected to a much more comfortable imprisonment.

As little as we know about Vlad's time spent in Hungarian captivity, there is an interesting tale from Russian chroniclers that discusses Vlad Dracula's favorite pastime during his time in prison.

This Russian source states, "It is said of him, however, that even when he was in jail, he did not cure himself of the evil habit of catching mice and buying birds at the market. He punished them by impaling them. He cut off the heads of some, others he had feathered and then allowed them to go. He learned to sew, and subsisted on that during his period of imprisonment." If any of this account is to be believed, one thing we can glean from it is that Dracula's imprisonment was one with substantial freedom. Because even in this gruesome narrative, it is indicated that Vlad was free to go to the market to buy birds. Someone confined to a dungeon at the bottom of Solomon's Tower would not be granted such a privilege. He was probably under simple under house arrest, likely under constant guard to prevent his escape.

After Dracula had spent about 12 years in this circumstance, the king of Hungary apparently had a change of heart, and decided that he just might prefer Dracula back on the throne of Wallachia after all.

He then determined to stipulate to Dracula what the terms of his aid would be. Among other things, his plan included Dracula's conversion from Eastern Orthodox Christianity to Roman Catholicism, and the marriage of Dracula to his sister. Dracula's choice was basically to either become a Catholic, marry the King of Hungary's sister, and reclaim his throne, or remain in prison and potentially be executed. For the pragmatic Dracula, whose religious beliefs never seemed to run too deep in the first place, the choice was abundantly clear.

He would don the vestments of the Catholics and marry a Hungarian princess in order to become the Prince of Wallachia once again. Immediately upon his agreement, Dracula was released and the wedding ceremony was arranged. Having apparently long forgotten about his Transylvanian bride who supposedly dove into the waters of Wallachia to escape an ill fate, Dracula attempted to forge a new future for himself with the hand that he had been dealt. The chroniclers date both Vlad Dracula's marriage and his release from prison to the year 1466. He would come to reclaim his throne for the third time in his life shortly thereafter.

The Return of the Dark Prince

Even after his release from prison and marriage to the king of Hungary's sister, not a lot is known of Vlad Dracula's time in that country. It is recorded that he had two sons, and mostly lived out a rather quiet existence as a subject of the Hungarian king. There is one anecdotal (and possibly even apocryphal) story from this time period involving a break-in at Dracula's Hungarian residence. According to the story, Dracula was more worried about the guard pursuing the thief than he was about the robber himself. Dracula supposedly lunged at the guard and killed him on the spot for trespassing.

When questioned about the incident Vlad is said to have simply remarked, "I did no evil; the captain is responsible for his own death. Anyone will perish thus who trespasses into the house of a great ruler. If this captain had come to me and had introduced himself, I would have found the thief and either surrendered him or spared him from death." Vlad opting to kill the pursuing guard for trespassing (rather than catching the thief) would indeed seem in line with what we know of Dracula's vengeful character, but the idea that the king would so easily sweep such a transgression under the rug seems a bit incredulous.

One thing we do know about this time period is that in Wallachia, Dracula's brother Radu was facing increasing opposition to his rule, both internally and abroad. He was viewed by all of his neighbors as a tool of the hated Turks who had placed him in power, so it wasn't long before powerful European rivals rose up to remove him. It was Stephen the Great, Dracula's cousin, who committed himself to this objective in the spring of 1473, in a confrontation over disputed territory in what is now the Ukraine.

Stephen would be victorious in this conflict, and would eventually lead the ouster of Radu from the Wallachian throne, replacing him with the son of Dan II, Basarab III (otherwise known as Basarab the Old). And although Dracula was momentarily passed up for the reclamation of the Wallachian throne, he was appointed a captain in the Hungarian army. Sometime in 1474 he was sent to lead a contingent of troops in the Transylvanian frontier. Here, in this troubled and often disputed region, it wasn't long before Dracula met his first engagement against the Turks, and he was involved in several skirmishes during the rest of 1474.

Then on January 10th, 1475, once again taking the side of his relative, Stephen the Great, Dracula joined forces with his army to fight the Turks in the Battle of Vaslui. This battle was actually set off when it was learned that Basarab III had betrayed the trust of Stephen the Great by entering into alliance with the Ottoman Turks, apparently repeating the same twisted political intrigue that had been plaguing Wallachian rulers for centuries. This then led to the predictable conflagration of European powers seeking to wrench yet another Wallachian tool of the Turks from power.

Of course Vlad Dracula was more than ready to take back his throne, and sought to do so, sidling right alongside Stephen the Great's army to finally reclaim his kingdom once and for all. As the Dracula coalition were in the midst of preparation for this final confrontation with Basarab, Dracula received official recognition as candidate for the Wallachian throne on January 21st, 1476. By February of 1476, Dracula's position was so strong that Basarab began to worry about pro-Dracula sentiment in the Transylvanian provinces north of Wallachia – so much so that he sent out an open letter to the citizens of the Transylvanian town of Sibiu, warning them that he wouldn't consider himself their friend as long as Dracula was living among them. The first few months of spring saw no actual military confrontations, however, and served as preparation time and a staging ground for the real offensive, which began in the summer months of 1476. Hungarian King Mathias had given supreme leadership of the Dracula coalition to a man named Stephen Bathory, a daring Balkan crusader who hailed from a rich family of Hungarian nobility.

As an interesting side note, Stephen's future niece, Elizabeth Bathory, would become infamously linked to vampirism in her own right several decades later, as the so-called "blood countess" who allegedly made it a routine habit of killing young peasant women, and then bathing in and drinking their blood.

Contrary to the future excesses of his niece, Stephen Bathory had no such proclivities. He was the supreme commander of the Wallachian campaign, but Dracula, being obviously much more experienced in the region, soon became the unofficial leader of the invasion force.

In an impromptu council of war held on July 25th, 1476, it was determined that the invasion force would consist of 15,000 Moldavians led by Stephen, attacking Wallachia from the east, while Dracula himself would lead a larger force of about 25,000 men, mostly Hungarians, Serbs, Transylvanians, and Wallachians, which would attack from the south.

The first battle was engaged on the outskirts of Wallachia in November of 1476. After scoring several early successes, the combined forces then reached the capital of the principality and overwhelmed it, capturing the main fortress on November 8th.

Clarifying their gains, Steven rattled off a letter which was sent on November 11th, stating that almost all of Wallachia was now in Dracula's hands. On November 26th it became official; Dracula was the ruler of Wallachia once again. This reign would prove to be much like his first, lasting for less than two months due to a lack of support – only this time Dracula himself would not survive. From the very moment of his reclamation he was placed in the precarious position of being foisted upon a populace of Wallachians who, remembering his previous atrocities against them, were not ready to welcome the despot back.

This internal pressure only compounded the obvious external threats of the Ottoman Turks, the remnants of the Basarab faction, and also neighboring Orthodox Christian Europeans, who basically viewed Dracula as an antichrist traitor for renouncing the Orthodox faith in favor of Catholicism. All of these enemies bided their time until Dracula's Hungarian protectors left the country. The moment his foreign protectors were gone, Vlad Dracula's growing crowd of antagonists were ready to strike him down.

The Death of Dracula?

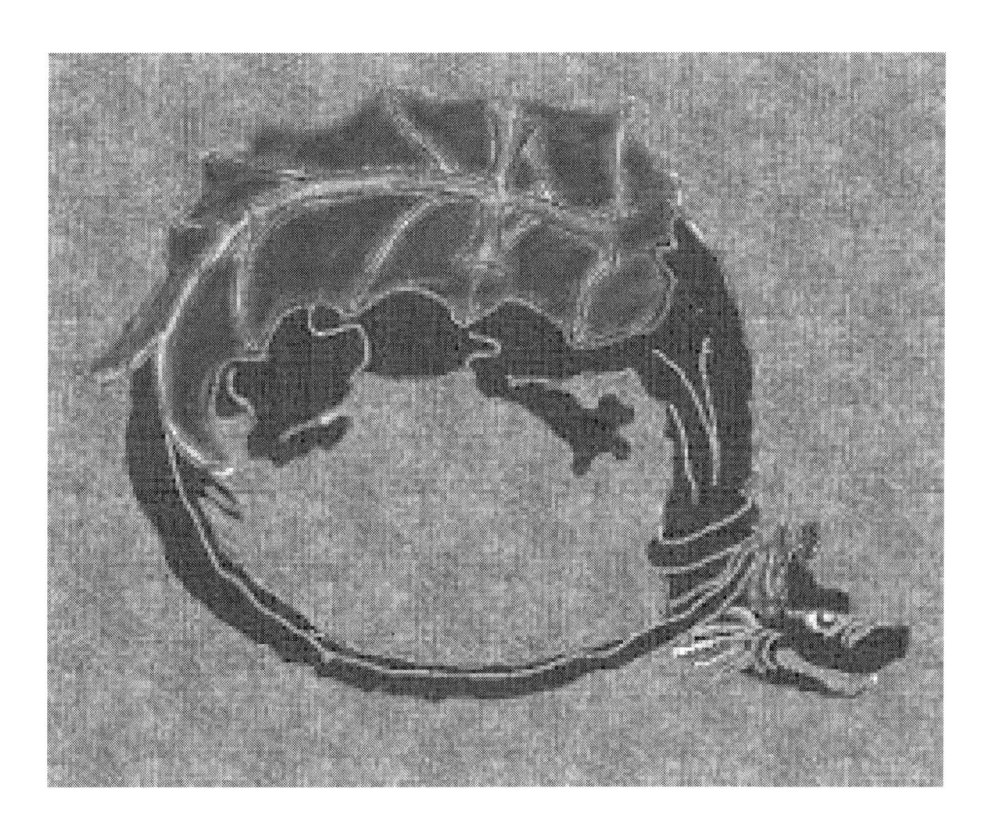

It is almost certain that Dracula had been deposed from his throne by January of 1477. Some mark his actual date of death a few weeks earlier, in December of 1476. But the manner of his demise has been open for debate ever since. Most contend that Dracula died in battle but there are competing tales as to just how this happened. Some Eastern European folklorists had spread the rumor that Dracula was actually killed by mistake, by his own soldiers who, in a bizarre onset of confusion, mistook Vlad Dracula for an infiltrating Turk.

According to this legend, Dracula's army was winning the battle against the Turks, had set them to flight, and Dracula and his men were in hot pursuit. It was then, when the remnants of this Turkish army were being butchered, that Vlad is said to have climbed up a mountain in order to see the action. According to the tale, in his excitement to get a good view of the carnage, Dracula became separated from his army. It was supposedly when one of his own scouts spotted him that the accident took place.

Mistaking Dracula for an enemy combatant, this scout launched a spear in Vlad Dracula's direction. This spear missed, but Dracula no doubt screamed a few choice obscenities in the wake of the attack. More of Dracula's troops then came to see what was causing the disturbance, and Dracula was so enraged at being set upon that he hurled himself at them, tearing into about five of the soldiers with his sword, hacking and slashing in a furious frenzy until they were all dead. This sudden reprisal on Vlad Dracula's part then drew the attention of some nearby archers, who promptly riddled the Wallachian Prince of Darkness with arrows, finally putting an end to his bloody reign.

This story has been told among Slavic communities in the Balkans for centuries, but has for the most part been dismissed as fiction.

Another version of events holds that Dracula stayed with his doomed contingent until the bitter end, and fought until his dying breath.

It is said that his corpse was then taken from a pile of dead bodies, his head cut off and handed over to the Turks. Dracula's head was then supposedly sent to Constantinople (modern day Istanbul) to display for Dracula's arch nemesis, the sultan, as evidence of his demise. Some locals have corroborated this legend to some extent, with a tale that seems to pick up where the Turkish one leaves off. According to this version of events, after the Turks rode off with Dracula's decapitated head, some of Dracula's few remaining faithful followers retrieved his headless body and had it buried in the nearby monastery of Snagov, which Dracula himself had founded.

According to this legend, his body remained hidden somewhere in this monastery. The local tradition held that Dracula had been buried right underneath the altar of the monastery so that the priests could continually pray over him. Investigating these long-held beliefs, an excavation team unearthed the remains in 1933. When the excavators dug underneath the altar, however, they were surprised to find a large hole, with no coffin or any other funerary refinement, simply bones at the bottom.

Upon closer examination, the bones proved to be mostly of animals, and were certainly not an indication of the final resting place of Vlad Dracula.

But then something interesting happened – archeologists uncovered a hidden, hitherto completely unknown tomb near the entrance of the monastery. There was no record of this tomb being created, and it was a mystery to everyone concerned. In contrast to the disordered pile of bones that had been discovered under the altar, upon opening this tomb, they found a well-preserved casket, covered in a princely purple shroud embroidered in expensive gold cloth.

Intrigued, the group carefully pried open the coffin to find the shattered remains of what had been a human skeleton. The bones were nothing more than fragments, and at first glance, it was exceedingly difficult to tell whether the skeleton had a head attached to it or not, making it difficult to corroborate the decapitated Dracula story one way or another. Lending support that the remains were those of Vlad Dracula, however, were the ornate silk vestments the deceased was wearing, still sharply recognizable amidst the dusty bone fragments of its former wearer.

With its ornate silver buttons, and gold-fringed, decorative colorings, this was clearly the clothing of someone important. And if the rich fabric of the skeleton's clothing wasn't a clear enough indication of royalty, the golden crown that was discovered by the remains served as a clear enough indication that this was the final resting place of some sort of potentate. The crown was encircled by ornate golden claws. Were these the claws of a dragon, as might indicate it was Dracula, the son of the dragon?

Many believe that this group of researchers did indeed uncover the tomb of Vlad Dracula. The prevailing theory to explain the long confusion over where the body was actually located was that the clergy had purposefully started the rumor that Dracula was buried under the alter as a kind of smokescreen, to divert attention away from the real burial spot. This was supposedly done to prevent the curious and grave robbers from disturbing the monarch's grave.

No explanation is given as to why the bones were in such poor condition…

There is a more recent interpretation of events however, that may offer an alternative explanation as to what happened to Dracula. New purported evidence gleaned by historians is creating a new narrative in which Vlad did not die in battle, as previously believed. According to this version, Vlad Dracula was actually captured alive, and taken back to Turkey in chains to meet the sultan.

It is said that Vlad's daughter Maria had married an Italian nobleman, and had by 1477 become the closest kin to her father. Therefore, it was she who entered into negotiations with the Ottoman Turks to gain her father's freedom. Experts hailing from the University of Tallinn have recently claimed to have found the documentation to prove that such bargaining for the life of Vlad Dracula did indeed take place. These documents reportedly indicate that Maria did pay a ransom, most likely raised by her husband's rich family, and successfully brought her father to Italy.

It is said that he died shortly thereafter and was buried at a monastery in Naples. These researchers have even claimed to have found Dracula's headstone at the church cemetery. It stands out because it is covered with imagery and symbols related to Transylvania, making it an extremely odd bedfellow when compared to its companions of standard Italian insignia. Most prominent of all, on this headstone is the depiction of a giant dragon, which of course seems to tie in with the Order of the Dragon.

The other thing that stands out is that on each side of this dragon are Egyptian-styled sphinxes. To the untrained eye it would seem odd to mix a smattering of Egyptian imagery in with Eastern European iconography, but experts in the field have concluded that when it comes to Vlad "Tepes" Dracula, it only makes sense. You see, the sphinx typically represents the city of Thebes, and Thebes is actually the Egyptian equivalent of Tepes, so the grave is actually adorned with imagery that corresponds with Vlad Tepes Dracula's two most well-known names.

But although many have chosen sides, and decided which one of these theories seems to be the best explanation for where Vlad Dracula's final, earthly resting place is, there are still many others who would disagree. Indeed, there are those who contend that *all theories* as to the mad monarch's place of burial are incorrect. There reason? They believe that this supposed vampire king of the undead never truly died…

Persisting Myths and Legends of Dracula

It's now over 500 years since Dracula's demise, and yet his legend is more alive than ever. Most of this acclaim can of course be directly attributed to Bram Stoker's 1898 depiction of the Eastern European monarch in his epic book, *Dracula*. But somewhere in between the historical Vlad Dracula and the works of fictitious literature and film there are persistent stories that some say prove there is yet more to this story that has never fully been told.

One of the more infamous conspiracy theories revolving around Vlad Dracula to come to light in recent decades is the one which connects Dracula to Judas Iscariot, the biblical betrayer of Christ. This legend has two variants. In one, Dracula is literally Judas, cursed with immortality shortly after the betrayal of Christ. Another version of the myth states that Judas was "father" of all vampires, and Dracula was merely one of the many descendants from this lineage.

The first variation of this undeniably far-fetched theory – that Dracula is Judas as an immortal, and has simply periodically changed his name and locale throughout the centuries – is a bit hard to swallow for even the most ardent of conspiracy theorists. Since Vlad Dracula's childhood under his father and then under the tutelage of the Ottoman Turks is fairly well documented, even for the most open mind, this would seem to be an irrefutable impossibility. If Judas was Dracula, how do you explain Vlad's childhood? Did this Judas Dracula spontaneously transform into a child in the 1400's and adopt Vlad Dracul II as his father? Even in the world of bizarre conspiracy theory, this narrative simply doesn't make any sense. At any rate, this piece of mythological theory is rather complicated, so before we delve into the so-called "evidences" that proponents of it point to, let's just relate the vampiric tale of Judas in its entirety.

This legend picks up where the biblical narrative of Judas leaves off. According to the official biblical canon, Judas betrayed Christ for 30 pieces of silver. Shortly after his betrayal, Judas felt horrible for what he had done and attempted to give the money back to the high priests of the Temple who had given it to him. But the priests refused to take it.

Judas then, in his frustration, hurled the silver on the ground and fled the temple in tears of despair. It is said that he then found a tree and hanged himself. This is where the traditional narrative ends. But according to the vampiric legend, after Judas tied that piece of rope around the tree branch, fastened the other end around his neck, and leapt down for a quick death, things did not go quite as he had planned. Immediately after his expiration, it is said that God brought Iscariot back to life, and cursed him to live as an undead immortal until the End Times.

Iscariot was revived, but he was not the same. It was said that he would no longer age or face conventional human sickness, and he would be virtually invulnerable to attack. But along with these supernatural "gifts," he would be unable to walk in full sunlight, as it would burn his skin, and he would be weakened to the point of death by silver, since it was 30 pieces of silver that he accepted to betray Christ. Furthermore, it is said that since life is in the blood, he would forever have an insatiable hunger for human blood.

All of these aspects of the story do conveniently fit in with the vampiric legends and lore that we all know and love, and it seems to connect perfectly with the larger Dracula story of Vlad Dracula living through the ages as an immortal since the time of Christ, or being at least descended from an ancient brood of immortal vampires. But really the question is whether any of this tale is based in reality at all. There have been rumors, and rumors of rumors, circulating on the internet for quite a few years now, stating that there is a mysterious extra biblical book called the *Book of Alugah* from whence this extra biblical vampiric mythology had sprung.

But beyond a few scant posts, "proof" of this supposed apocryphal text is rather scarce. All references say that the book was written by a Catholic monk named Aed around 843 A.D., but without hard data backing it up, this could all be made up.

There really is an extra biblical book of proven voracity called the *Gospel of Judas*. This book is a so-called "Gnostic Gospel" produced by the 2nd century sect of Christians who practiced Christian Gnosticism. The word *gnostic* translates from the Greek, and means *knowledge*. This sect sought to reinterpret many of the traditional beliefs of 1st century Christians. One of these reinterpretations was the role of Judas in the gospel narrative. Said to have been written around 200 A.D., this book diverges drastically from the traditional Christian view of Judas as an unforgivable betrayer, and instead paints him as a most understanding and adept disciple of Christ, who played a vital role in Christ's ministry.

While it certainly does portray the traditional biblical narrative – especially the nature and role of Judas – it does so in a dramatically different light, and it hardly mentions anything about him being a vampire!

But if you think this tale of Dracula Judas is out of this world, it's nothing in comparison to the conspiracy theory straight out of the ancient alien camp, which contends that Vlad Dracula may have somehow been (no I'm not kidding) a blood-sucking alien from outer space.

This whole UFO hullabaloo began when an odd, never-before-seen tapestry was uncovered in Vlad Dracula's supposed birthplace, which seemed to depict an alien spacecraft. There in the painting was some sort of saucer-shaped vehicle hovering over Transylvanian rooftops, emitting what appeared to be smoke.

It was from this single image that ancient astronaut theorists came up with an entire backstory for Vlad the space alien. They seemed to believe the smoking craft must have crashed somewhere in the region, and the escaping aliens survived through the centuries by sustaining themselves with blood. A bit reaching, you might say?

As much as we might want to scoff at such seemingly outrageous claims, there is one further anecdote of interest when it comes to the alleged UFO connection to Romania. Recently, the Romanian government has revealed that a very odd metal structure was recovered in Vlad Dracula's old stomping grounds that seems to defy the historic record. This piece of metal was actually discovered in 1973, but due to the strict communist Iron Curtain that Romania was under at the time, it was locked away and kept secret.

The ongoing research into this mystery metal has now been released, and it has been revealed that the metal is made of a sophisticated aluminum composite, produced some 250,000 years ago! The piece shows all indications of being artificially made, and so no rational explanation exists to account for what this artifact is or where it comes from. And so, to quote the illustrious Ancient Astronaut proponent George Tsoukalos, "I'm not saying it's aliens…but it's aliens!"

Another real-life vampire legend connected with Dracula in particular, and the region of Transylvania in general, is *Hoia Baciu*. This thick forest, located right in the middle of Transylvania, has been the hotbed of strange and unusual paranormal activity for quite some time. Even the terrain is odd, with the trees being thick around the edges of the woods before abruptly thinning to a wide-open clearing in the center. This fact in itself has led some to speculate that there is a reason for that clearing. And for an explanation, some look to Dracula himself.

Some have claimed that the reason no tree dares to take root on this particular plot of land is because this is where Vlad Dracula is buried. But this (as is the case with many paranormal sites) is only one among countless theories offered for the paranormal activity said to be present. Furthermore, the tales of strange activity in the forest most likely predate the time of Dracula.

According to local folklore the forest gets its name from a local shepherd, and 200 of his sheep, who went missing here. Indeed, the Romanian word for shepherd is *baci*, so the tale does appear to have some sort of connection to the forest's mythology. According to the legend, the locals searched the forest for several days after the disappearance, but no one ever found any trace of the shepherd, or recovered even one of his 200 sheep! It was as if they had just winked out of existence. In the years since this event, there have been countless more disappearances of a similar nature, with people going into the forest, but never coming out.

That is, except for one instance that allegedly occurred a few decades ago, in which a local five-year-old girl wandered into the haunted forest, and returned several years later. This girl, like the others, was seen to go into this cursed patch of trees, and was never seen to come out – that is, until five years later! But that isn't even the strangest part. The really odd part of this tale is that although five years had passed for everyone else, no time at all seemed to have elapsed for the returned, missing girl. She was not only the same age, but she was wearing the same clothing with no sign of wear or tear after all that time!

Upon being questioned, the girl appeared to have no idea whatsoever where she had been during the past five years. It was as if she were either frozen in time, or perhaps even *transported* in time, five years into the future in a matter of seconds. For her, one second it was 1965, and then one magical snap of the enchanted forest's fingers later, it was instantly 1970!

Since the Middle Ages it has been speculated that at the heart of this forest lies a doorway to other worlds, allowing hapless human wanderers to slip into them, and other *more frightful entities* to slip out.

Mysterious disappearances are just the tip of the iceberg when it comes to the strangeness of this Transylvanian landmark. Since the late 1960s there have been several UFO sightings, and strange "glowing orbs" have been said to have been seen on a daily basis. The gnarled trees that grow so stunted, as if under the oppression of an unseen force or energy, also play into the oddity of Hoia Baciu, with brave visitors who have spent the night claiming that the trees themselves take on the appearance of tortured human beings, often appearing as if they are tied or *impaled* on wooden stakes!

Yes, if you haven't guessed it already, this is the other strange happening of Hoia Baciu that links back to Vlad the Impaler. You see, there is a legend around this haunted forest stating that thousands of peasants were slaughtered in a massacre by Dracula on this very spot. Could it be the atrocities committed by Vlad Dracula that have caused this land to become so horribly cursed?

Or are we to believe that this strange wood is Vlad Dracula's burial ground, and his evil and all of the strife and discord he carried with him in life are manifest here in death? There are also those who believe that the very reason Transylvania has so many myths and legends of monsters, weird creatures, and yes, vampires, is because there exists a portal to another dimension located right in the center of this dark, enchanted forest.

According to them, this is the astral revolving door through which the bogeyman, werewolves, vampires, and many other nasties periodically waltz, in order to visit our world. Of course, this is all just a theory. Probably.

The Compelling Haunting of Dracula

Even before Bram Stoker's epic work entitled *Dracula* the historical figure behind the fiction had been the focal point of morbid fascination for centuries. It was quite easy for Stoker to imbue Vlad Tepes with the frightful imagery found in Romanian folktales about blood sucking creatures, because of how bloodthirsty this tyrannical monarch truly was in real life. Vlad Tepes or Vlad Dracula, whichever name you which to use, was the perfect template on which to pen such a character.

He was not only a power mad, demonic despot who ruled his people with an iron fist, he was also the tortured, misunderstood soul who had suffered immensely much of his own life. As it stands, if one didn't have to consider all the victims that Vlad is alleged to have impaled (some reports are as high as 100,000) you almost can't help but feel sorry for him. He was born into not only a dysfunctional family, but a dysfunctional nation, in which life, liberty, and limb were constantly under siege.

His father's kingdom, like a traditional victim in vampire lore, was having the lifeblood squeezed out of it by both over-ambitious rulers in Hungary to the north, and the powerful Muslim sultan of the Ottoman Empire to the south. Vlad's father was forced to maneuver constantly between two empires threatening to snuff his kingdom out of existence. And when his father could no longer effectively play both ends of this dangerous high-stake game of Wallachian Craps, he was forced to roll the dice, and gamble his own children as collateral.

It was as a hostage of the Ottomans that Vlad Dracula learned just how cheap and meaningless life could be, as he lived with the constant threat of death hanging right over his head. It is here, it is fairly safe to say, that Dracula first began to devalue the lives of others, as well as his own. And after his release from this perilous bondage, when he was given his chance to reign and control his own kingdom, he sought to enforce his own warped sense of justice, which he had developed during his captivity.

As bad as Dracula may seem to us (and there is no denying his atrocities), during his final battles against the Turks, Vlad viewed himself as Christian Europe's only hope, the only ruler fierce enough to halt the Ottoman advance. Many Romanians also understand that the times Vlad ruled in were in a way different than today and recognize his efforts to preserve the people and their identity against overwhelming odds.

It seems that Dracula – both Stoker's fictional vampire, and the real-life monarch – is a figure that both repels and attracts us at the same time. There is something about the dark figure of Dracula that we cannot resist, even though we know we should. This enigma of warped personality, this vampiric Prince of Darkness still alternately compels and haunts us all, to this very day.

Also by Conrad Bauer

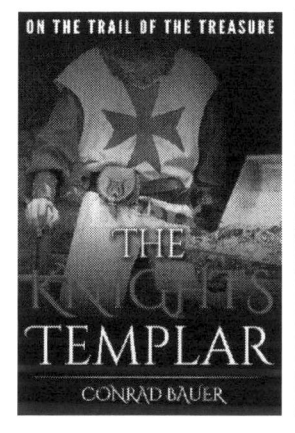

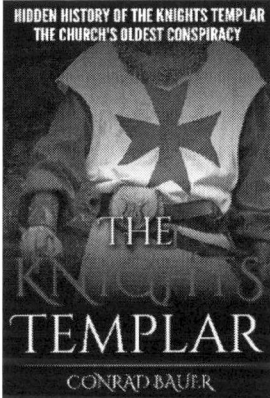

CONRAD BAUER
OPUS DEI
CATHOLICISM'S SECRET SECT
SECRET SOCIETIES

HISTORY'S GREATEST SPIES
The Hidden Story of
RICHARD SORGE
CONRAD BAUER

CONQUERORS OF THE WORLD
The Vikings
CONRAD BAUER

THE HIDDEN HISTORY OF THE CRUSADERS AND THE CONSPIRACIES THAT FOLLOWED
The
CRUSADES
CONRAD BAUER

A BEGINNER'S GUIDE TO
ARCHANGELS
Conrad Bauer

NEAR DEATH
Experiences
The Truth Revealed
CONRAD BAUER

THE STRANGE & UNEXPLAINED MYSTERIES OF THE WORLD
THE BERMUDA
TRIANGLE
THE TRUTH REVEALED
CONRAD BAUER

NEAR DEATH
Experiences
VOL. 2
The Truth Revealed
CONRAD BAUER

Modern Tales
of the
Unexplained
CONRAD BAUER

PARANORMAL
CREATURES
Investigating Cryptozoology
CONRAD BAUER

HAUNTED
PLACES
CHILLING PARANORMAL AND SUPERNATURAL
GHOST STORIES FROM AROUND THE WORLD
CONRAD BAUER

THE MOST
TERRIFYING PLACES
ON EARTH
Searching Through the
World's Most Horrifying
and Scary Locations
CONRAD BAUER

Paranormal UFO Sighting Cases that
Still Mystify Non-Believers
ALIENS
CONRAD BAUER

TUNGUSKA
AN APOCALYPTIC EVENT
BEYOND BELIEF
CONRAD BAUER

SHERGAR
A True Crime Story of Kidnapping,
Racehorse, and Politics
CONRAD BAUER

Further Readings

Now that you have finished reading about the history and legend of Dracula, I just wanted to take the time to share with you some of the sources that have proved invaluable in the writing of this book. Here you will find all of the snippets of information and facts – as well as myths and legends – that helped make this book possible.

<u>In Search of Dracula, Raymond T. McNally & Radu Florescu</u>
This book is perhaps one of the most popular of all of the books written by the Romanian researcher Radu Florescu. In it, he, along with Raymond T. McNally, help to uncover some of the lesser-known aspects of the real-life Dracula's history. The book not only provides a clear and concise timeline of events in Vlad Dracul's life, it also helps us to understand the backdrop against which these events played out. The treacherous and perilous world of politics in Eastern Europe is explained in a manner that perhaps only someone who grew up in Romania himself could clearly convey.

One of the best things about this epic treatise on Dracula is the manner in which it separates fact from fiction, but then goes back to find relevant links that the historical Vlad Dracula may have had with rampant Romanian folklore, which later proved to be such fertile soil for the imagination of Bram Stoker's *Dracula* hundreds of years later. If you are interested in Dracula – fact, fiction, and everything in between – this book is a must read!

Dracula: A Biography of Vlad the Impaler 1431-1476, Radu Florescu & Raymond T. McNally

Here is another great book by Radu Florescu and Raymon T. McNally. Written in 1973, this book was the seminal source of information on Dracula as the excitement around the 1976, 500th anniversary of Vlad's death neared. This book, true to form, does indeed offer a fairly clear picture of Vlad's life from 1431 to 1476. But as good as this book is, there is one common complaint in how it is written. For some odd reason, there are several quotations from historical sources offered throughout the book, in languages such as Latin, German, and Romanian, that offer no translation.

If you do not happen to know these languages, they are basically meaningless quotes for the reader. Time and time again, you will find passages that leave the reader linguistically guessing. I'm not sure what purpose this serves, since the reader is unable to ascertain what the quote conveys. It almost seems like an error, as if editors were meant to translate them, but failed to do so.

The book has been in print for decades, however, and this oddity has never changed. Thankfully for readers today, just a quick query with Google translate will help clear up most of these aberrations, but it is still an odd aspect of this book nevertheless. All in all, the vast bulk of the information found in *Dracula: A Biography of Vlad the Impaler* is reliably sound, and well worth your time.

Dracula: Prince of Many Faces – His Life and Times, Radu Florescu and Raymond T. McNally

Yet another great book from Radu Florescu and Raymond T. McNally. Written in 1988, this book serves as a veritable treasure trove of all things vampire and all things Dracula. Just as the title might imply, *Dracula: Prince of Many Faces* seeks to show the many sides of Dracula, and present aspects of his history from perspectives that the reader may not be aware of. If you would like a clear and non-biased view of the man who became Dracula, then you might want to keep a copy of this book on your bookshelf.

Dracula's Wars: Vlad the Impaler and his Rivals, James Waterson

This book approaches the Dracula saga from the perspective of the many military engagements he fought. Military strife was a major part of Dracula's life. He was literally born into it, inheriting the military order of his father, the order of the "Dragon," from which his name was derived. This book seeks to examine all of the intricacies of these military engagements, their motivations, side effects, and ultimate outcomes. If you would like a book that has a play by play of every battle that Prince Vlad Dracula was ever a part of, then Dracula's Wars should be your go-to source of information.

Dracula. Matei Cazacu

Cazacu is a preeminent Dracula historian who wrote his famed master's thesis, *Vlad the Impaler: A Historical Monograph* for the University of Bucharest all the way back in 1969. Standing shoulder to shoulder with other Dracula heavyweights such as Radu Florescu and Raymond T. McNally, Cazacu is more than well-read when it comes to the subject. Here in this book he gives us a unique take on the Dracula history, and phenomenon as a whole. Utilizing a top-down approach, he leaves no stone unturned when it comes to the Dracula narrative. This is a must-read.

***Real Vampires, Night Stalkers, and Creatures from the Darkside*, Brad Steiger**

Mr. Steiger is a true authority when it comes to myths and legends of all kinds, and this book has been an invaluable resource when it comes to piecing together some of the more obscure legends circulating around Dracula. This book provides not only great details about the mythology of Dracula but also other lesser known vampires such as Elizabeth Bathory and several others. If you would like to beef up your knowledge on the folktales and legends on which much of the Dracula mythos is based, this book would serve as more than a good start for you!

***The Werewolf Book: The Encyclopedia of Shape Shifting Beings*, Brad Steiger**

This is another Brad Steiger paranormal *tour de force* and here you can find even further anecdotal tales on vampires, and other strange paranormal creatures claimed to run rampant in our world. All of these stories are, of course, to be taken with a grain of salt, but whether they are real or fantasy, they serve as a great window into the mindset of the mythmaking endemic in places like Dracula's Transylvania. This massive compendium of the frightening, bizarre, and just plain odd, was an invaluable resource for this book. It's a real page turner, and well worth a read.

www.mysteriousuniverse.org

This site proved to be a great resource when it came to some of the more recent myths and legends in regard to Dracula. If you would like to learn more about claims of Dracula's final resting place, and learn more of strange places in the

Transylvanian/Wallachian region of Romania, this site has everything you need!

Image Credits

Did Dracula Really Exist? - https://pxhere.com/en/photo/66824

The Precarious Childhood of Dracula - https://pixabay.com/en/bat-dracula-silhouette-mammal-24578

Map of Wallachia and Transylvania - By Spiridon Ion Cepleanu (Own work) [CC BY-SA 4.0 via Wikimedia Commons

Dracula and the Tightrope of Leadership
https://commons.wikimedia.org/wiki/File:Vlad_tepes_painting.jpg

Dracula Takes Back his Throne
https://commons.wikimedia.org/wiki.File:Ivan_Yermenov_Singing_beggars.jpg

Beating the Drums of War - https://commons.wikimedia.org/wiki/File:Vlad_Tepes_XIX.jpg

The Dragon's Crusade - https://en.wikipedia.org/wiki/Saint_George_and_the_Dragon

Vlad Dracula's Escape
https://commons.wikimedia.org/wiki/File:Vlad_Tepes_-Master_of_Maria_am_Gestade.jpg

The Death of Dracula? - https://commons.wikimedia.org/wiki/File:Dragon_order_insignia.jpg

Persisting Myths and Legends of Dracula
- https://commons.wikimedia.org/wiki/File:Turnul_Chindiei_-_Cetatea_de_scaun_Targoviste.jpg

Printed in Great Britain
by Amazon